Mi'ani'festo

Poems are energy.

And pwoermds are the smallest, talismanic scraps of energy. They leave the barest suggestion of meaning that the reader can interpret, spin-off, double-read, see and then see again— but most of the time they refuse even that, and I love them for it. They are fragments; they are essence; they are spells.

The glass poems I have made are haptic poems that began as pwoermds. Over time, I reworked these clandestine and evocative pieces into physical objects meant to be handled, turned about in the hands, held up to light and experienced. The photographs in this collection replicate this experience of handling and seeing, and duplicate the variations of this experience.

Because they are glass, they are never the same experience twice. Because most of them are made with dichroic glass— a variety of glass which displays two or more different colors in certain lighting conditions— this variety is even more pronounced. Dichroic glass is wonderfully gaudy and transient, a passionate and lively material, filled with fugitive colors that change and engage playfully throughout the day, depending on the angle of view, the light, the weather, or even what is reflected, sky, face, or earth.

I love glass because it is inherently responsive. Lively and reflective by nature, it participates in the environment. It doesn't exclude the world around it. It can't help itself. It fits these pwoermds because they too invite participation, never settling on meaning.

Mirrors always reflect something, even when nothing is there, and glass is the eye taking you in and seeing you right back. I believe mirrors hold history and record the soul. When I see myself reflected, I am speaking to the past, to the ghosts who once gazed as I gaze..

These pieces are therefore participatory— they're brevity invites and provokes thought, emotion, and memory. This is a part of their life, their depth, their jouissance.

I want to offer my special and heartfelt thanks to Sadie for her expert advice on the nature of glass, assistance with the engineering, and for kindly giving me her dichroic glass remnants. This work would have been a lot more difficult without her help.

Thanks especially to mIEKAL aND for helping to make sassafracas— the pieces of which now reside in a box and await glass-fusing, the next incarnation of object making that will break the colors up into glittering stars— become an object I can share with the world.

With Love, Suzanne Mercury

ISBN-10: 1-936687-45-3
ISBN-13: 978-1-936687-45-9

Xerolage 69 First Edition published 2018   ISSN 1557-0983
Visual poetry, copy art & collage graphics, each issue devoted to the work of one artist. Xerolage is a word coined by mIEKAL aND to suggest the world of 8.5 x 11 art propagated by xerox technology. "The mimeo of the 80s." The primary investigation of this magazine is how collage technique of 20th century art, typography, computer graphics, visual & concrete poetry movements & the art of the xerox have been combined. 8.5x11, 84 pages each. Subscriptions $24/4 issues. For overseas delivery, add $15 for airmail printed matter.

Back issues $6.00 each.

Xexoxial Editions, 10375 Cty Hway Alphabet, LaFarge, WI 54639
www.xexoxial.org | perspicacity@xexoxial.org

aci'ga
Honeycomb variation, dichroic glass against steel with glass dust halo

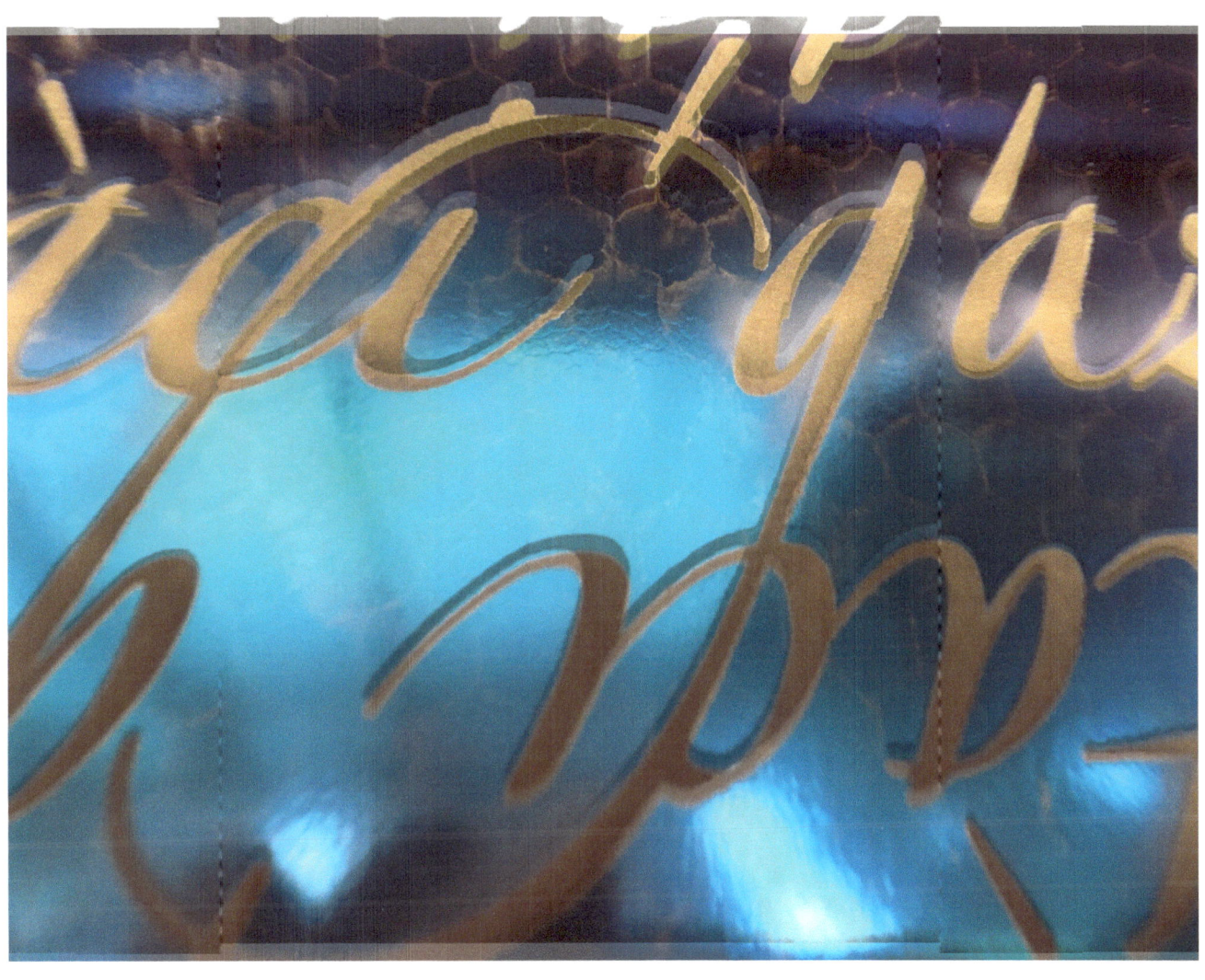

Jouisseance
Reverse side of mirror, in a shadowbox lit up from behind

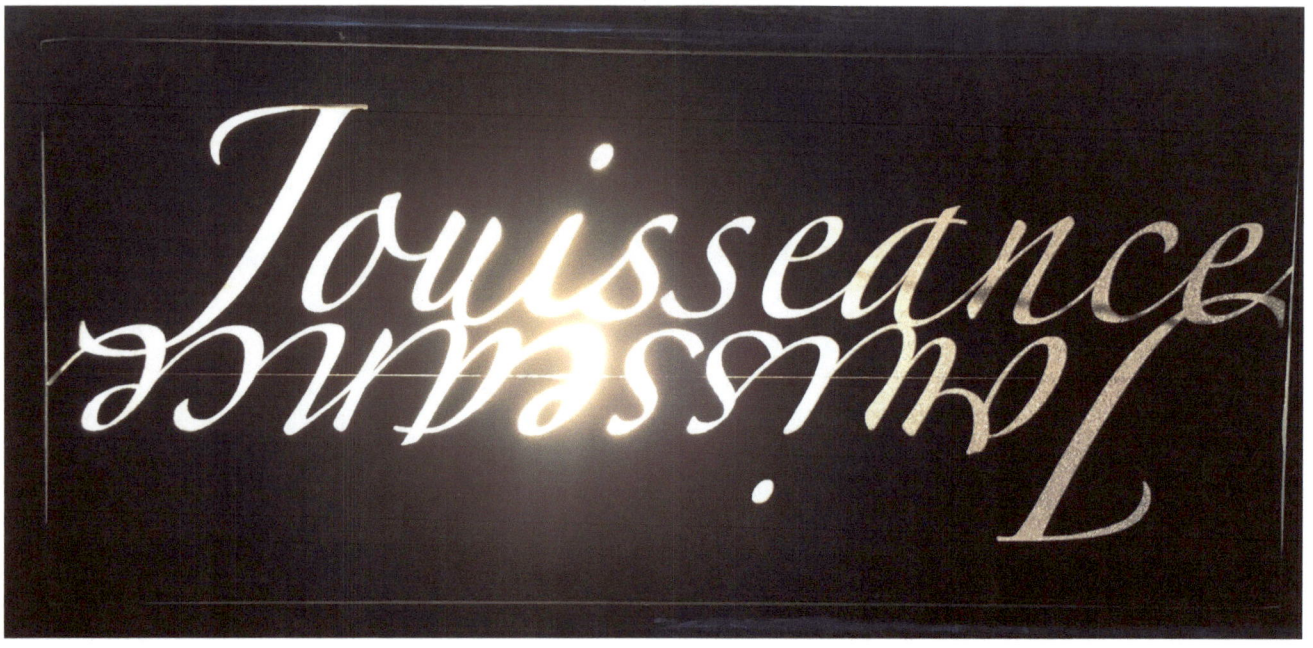

citaci'gazze
Variation in cerulean and jade, dichroic glass on earth reflecting sky with self-portrait

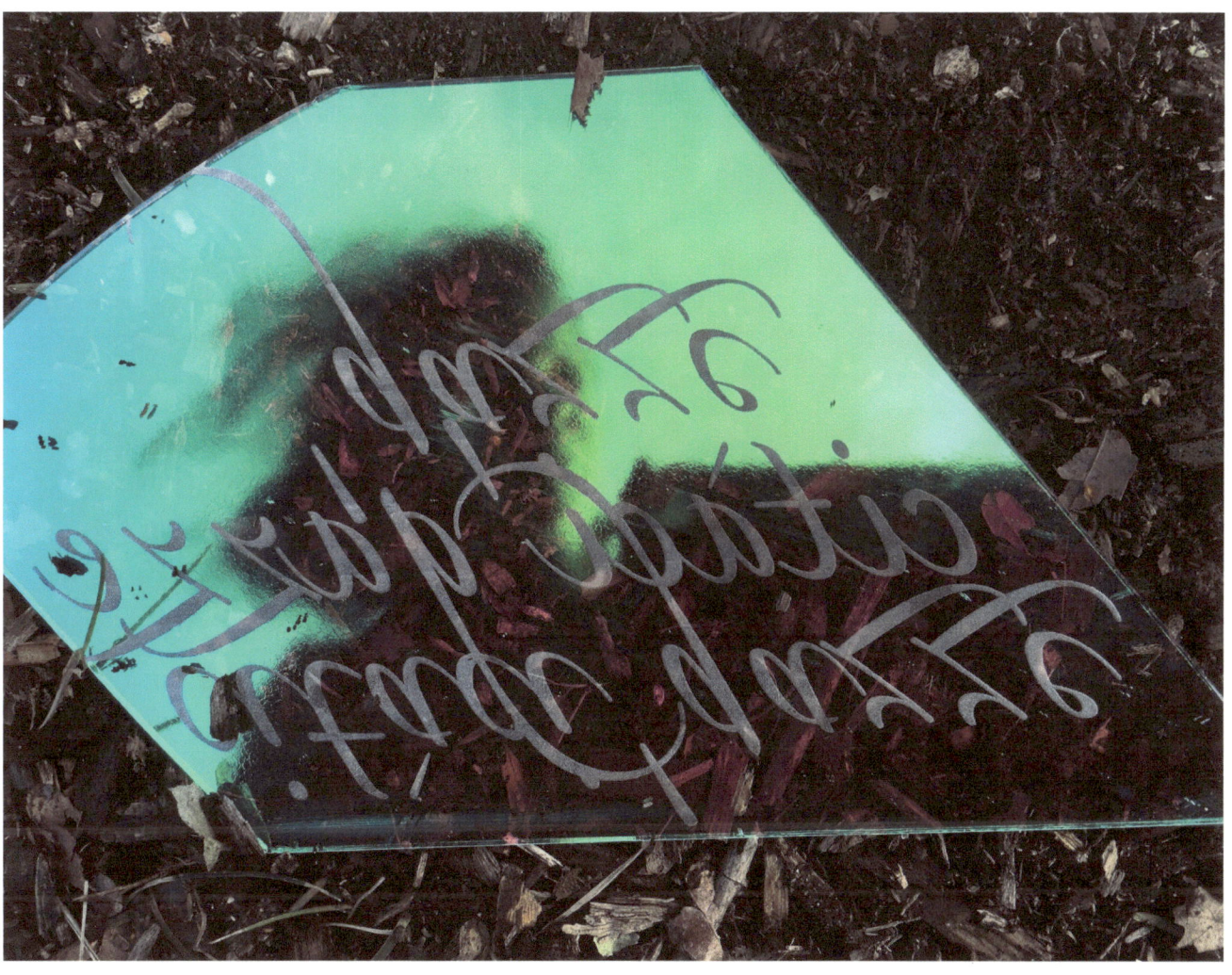

Suzanne Mercury

sassafraeas, variation #1
Seaglass variation, dichroic glass against gravestone marble

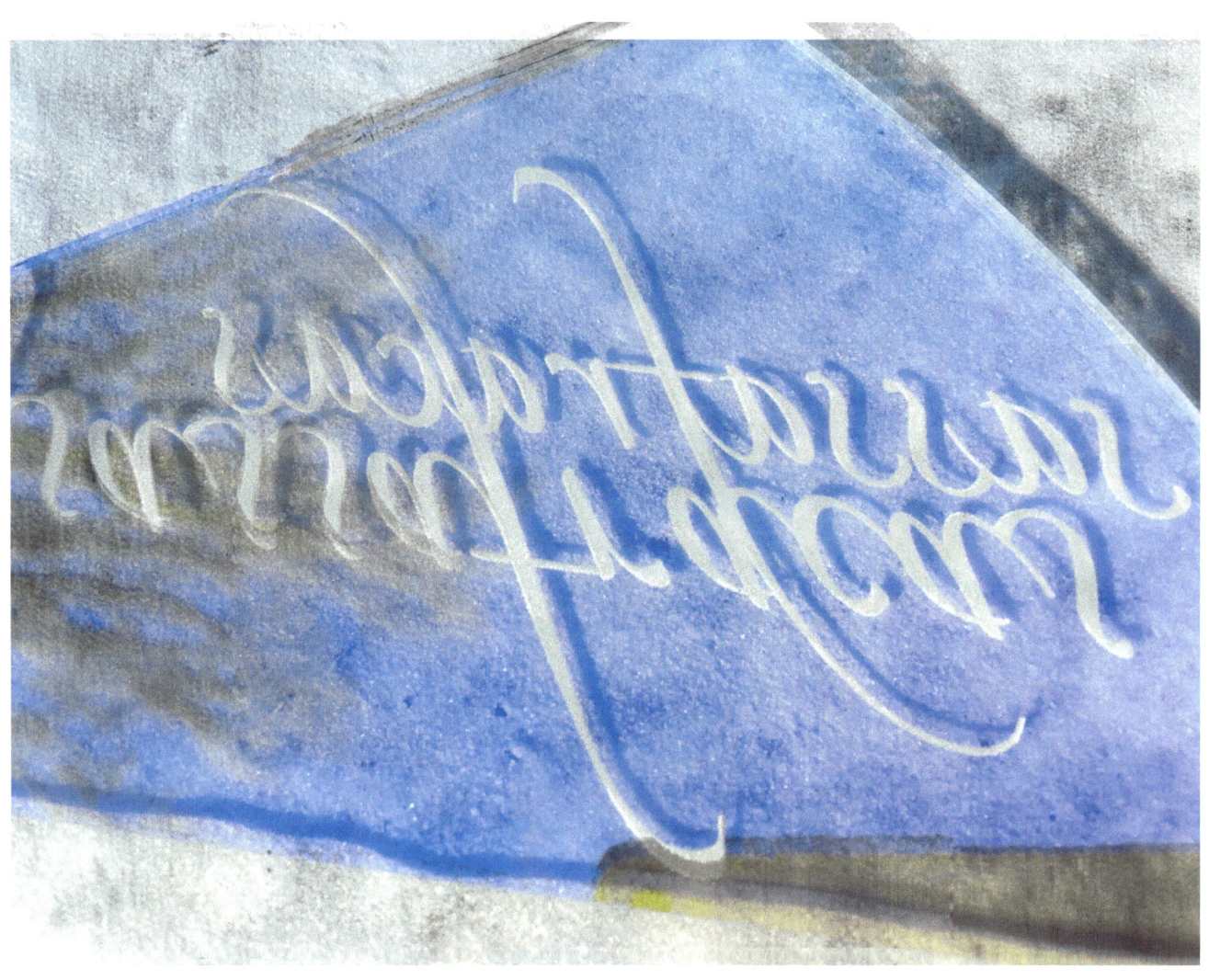

felicitail, variation #1

Sunrise variation, dichroic glass reflecting early morning sky against gravestone marble

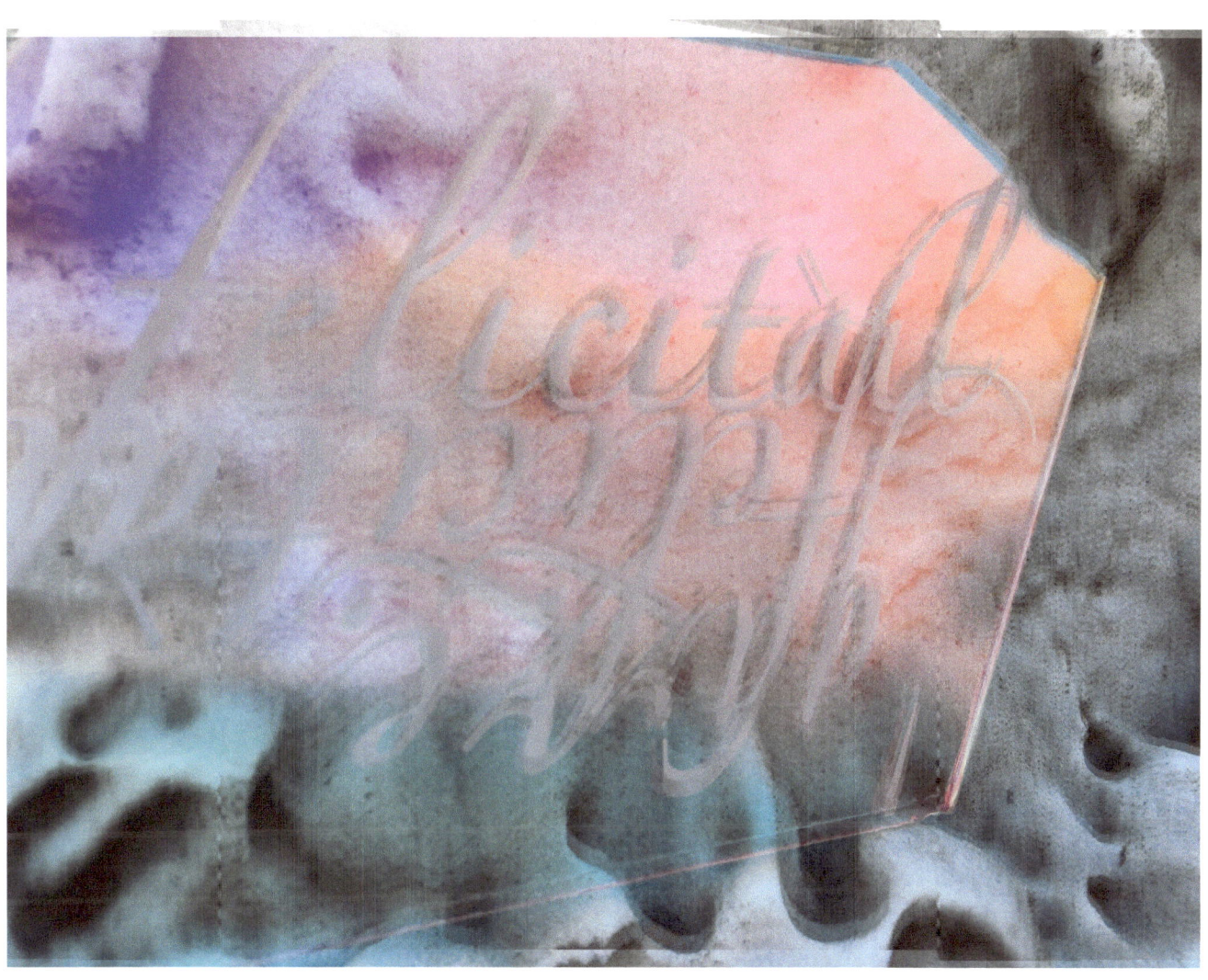

Melonight, variation #1
Fuschia variation, dichroic glass with raindrops, hands, and houseplants

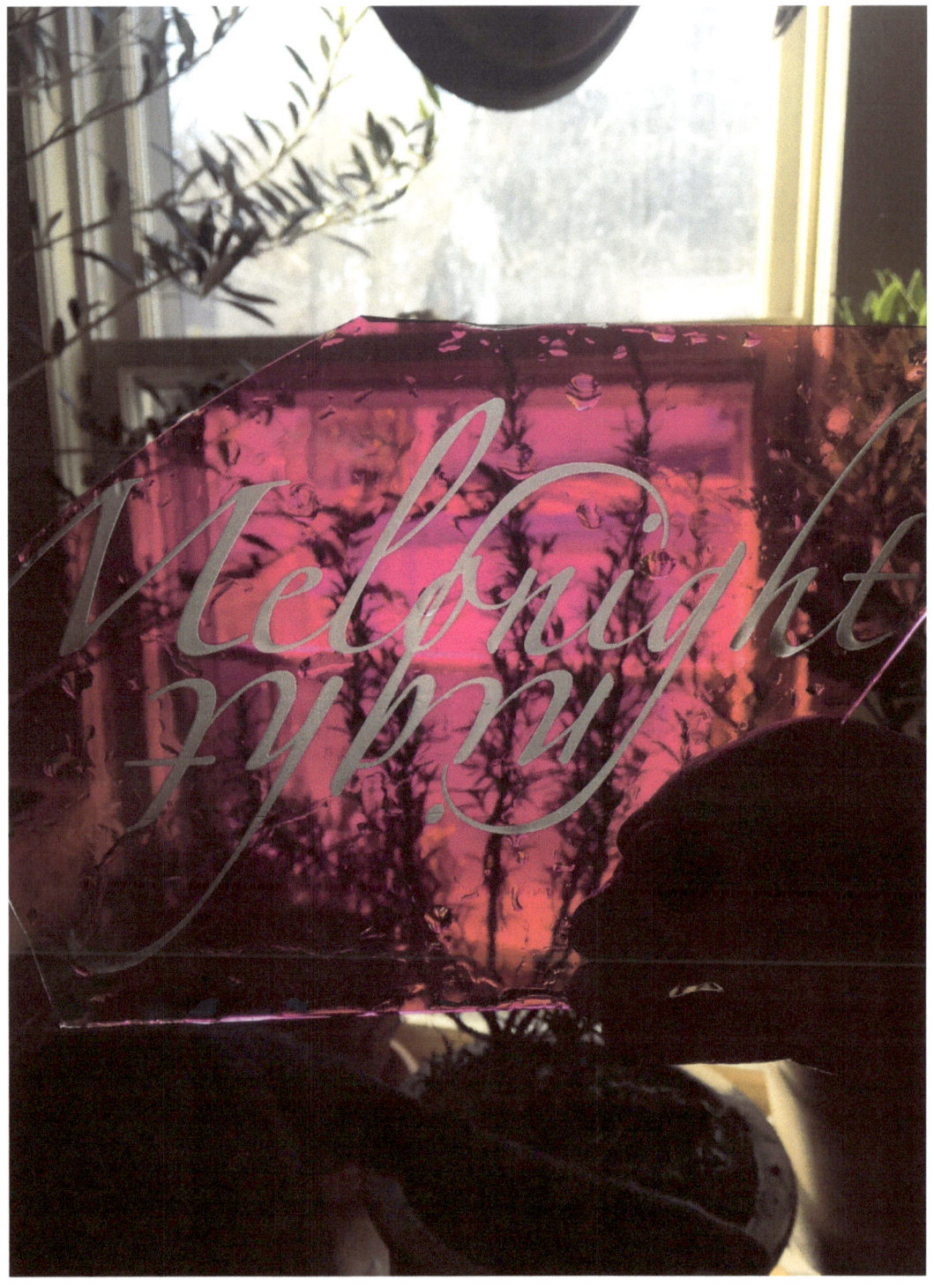

knickerfluff, variation #1
Cobalt variation, dichroic glass against yew tree reflecting sky and tree branches

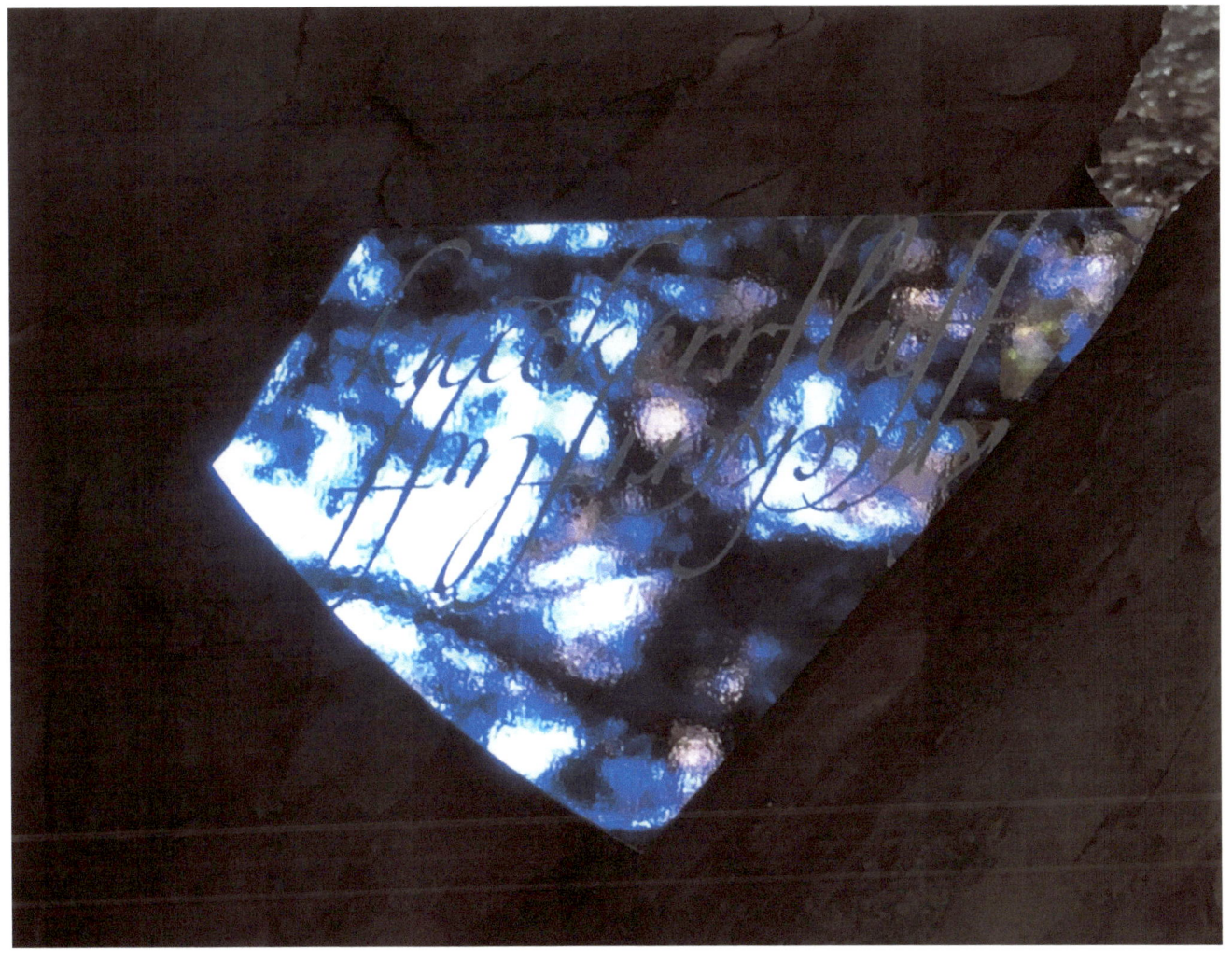

Suzanne Mercury

Asphodelerium
Reverse side of mirror, washed in acid, in a shadowbox

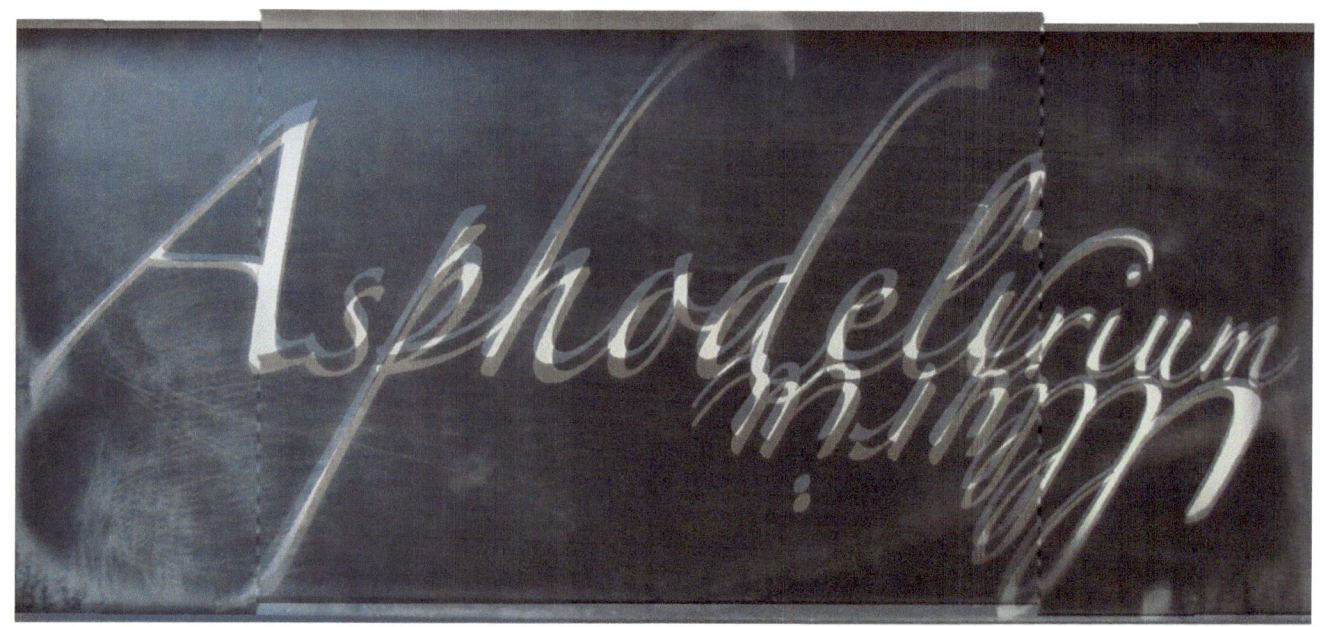

felicitail, variation #2
Honeycomb apple variation, dichroic glass against steel with gold and glass dust halo

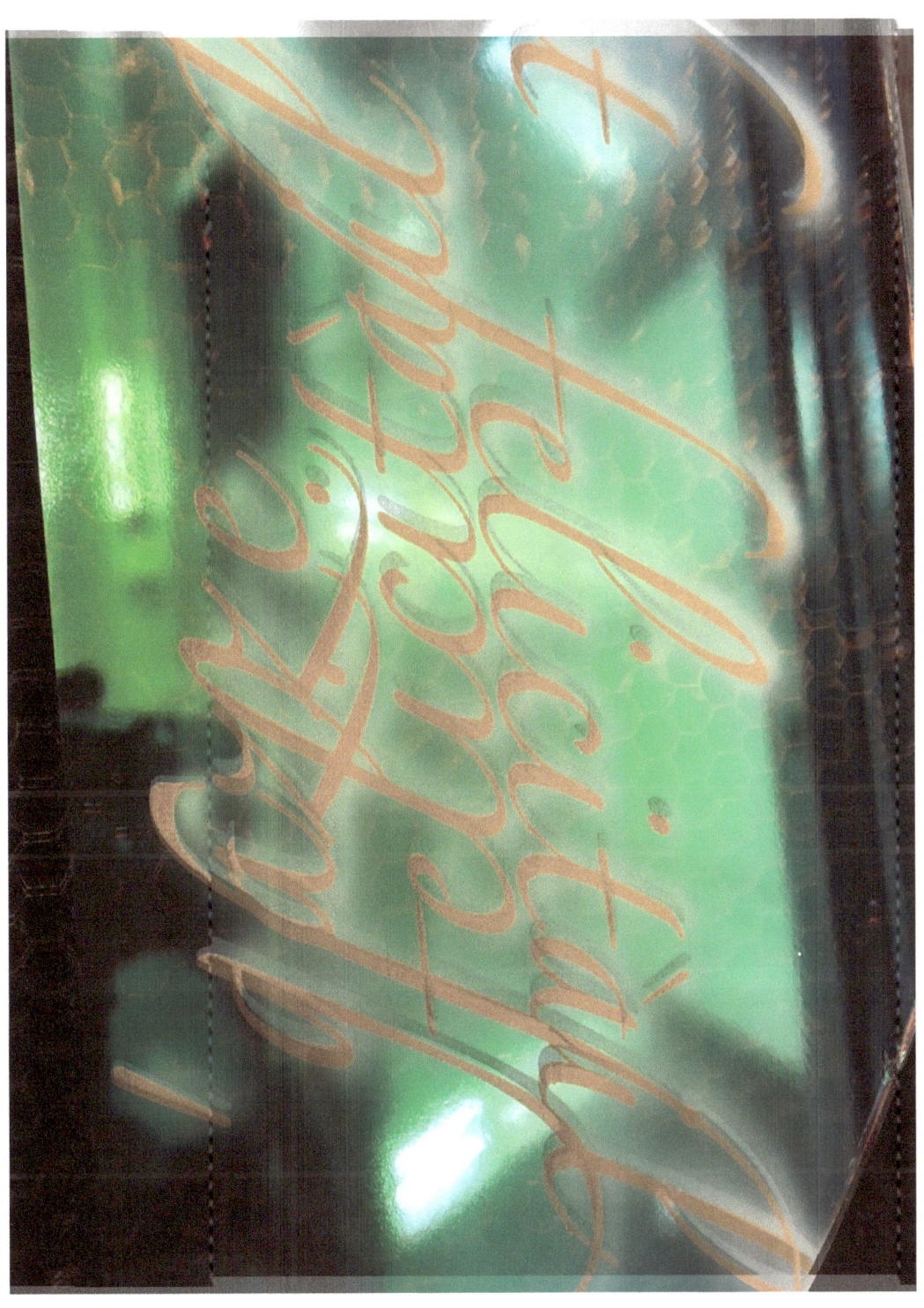

Xaphania, variation #1
Azure variation, dichroic glass reflecting sky against granite gravestone

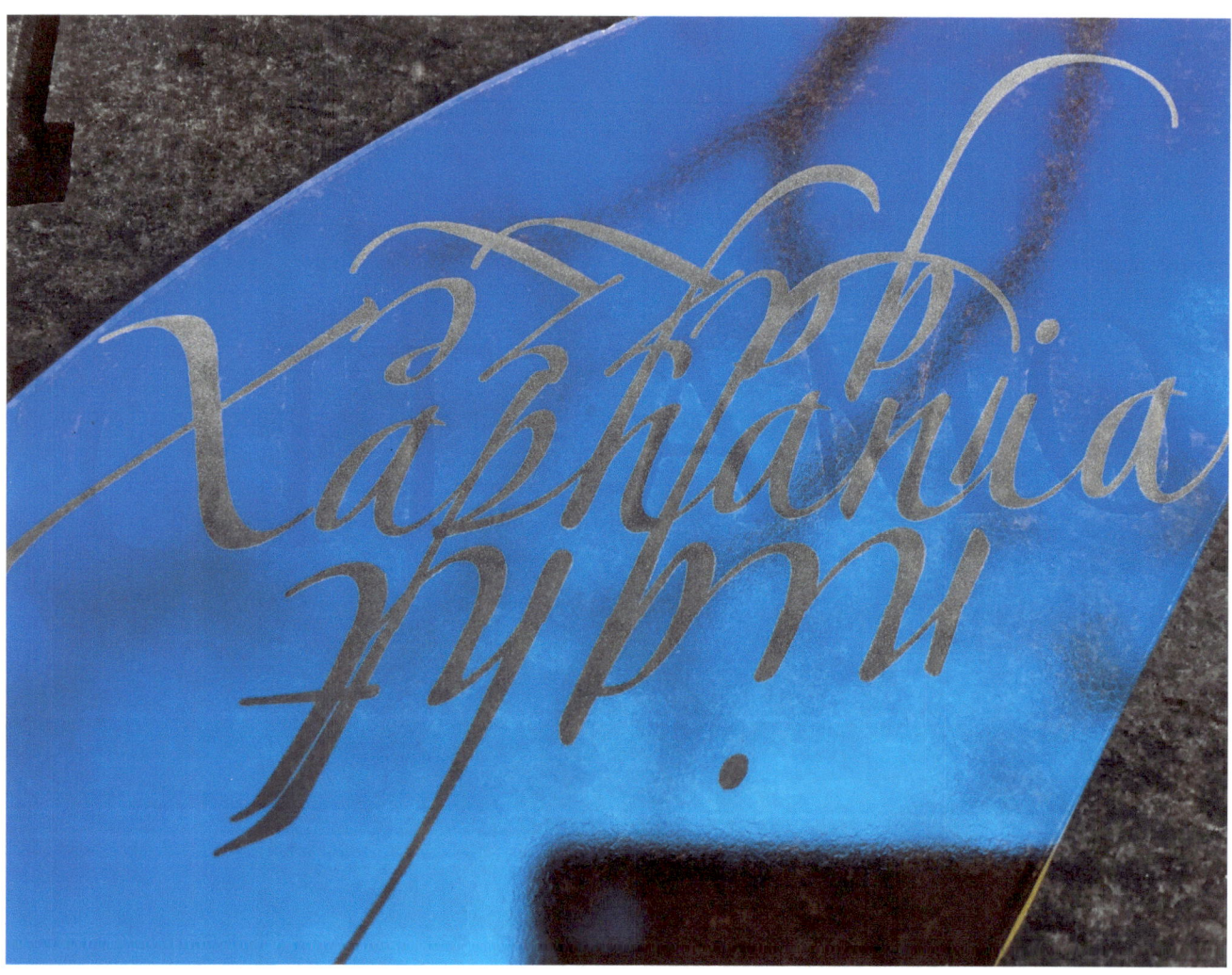

knickerfluff, variation #2
Honeycomb variation in grey green, dichroic glass against steel with gold leaf and glass dust halo

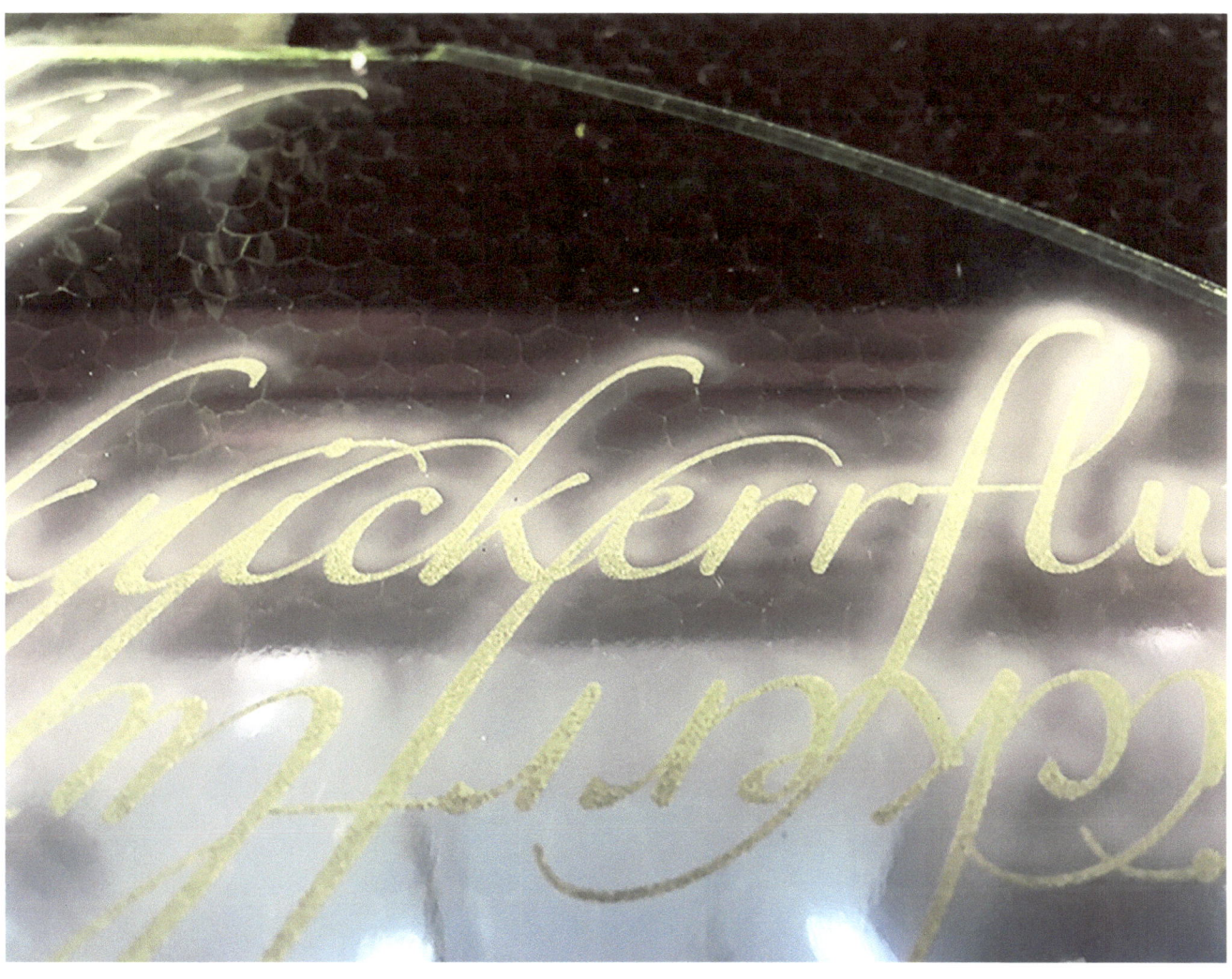

felicitail, variation #3
Hot pink variation, dichroic glass on garden soil reflecting the evening sky

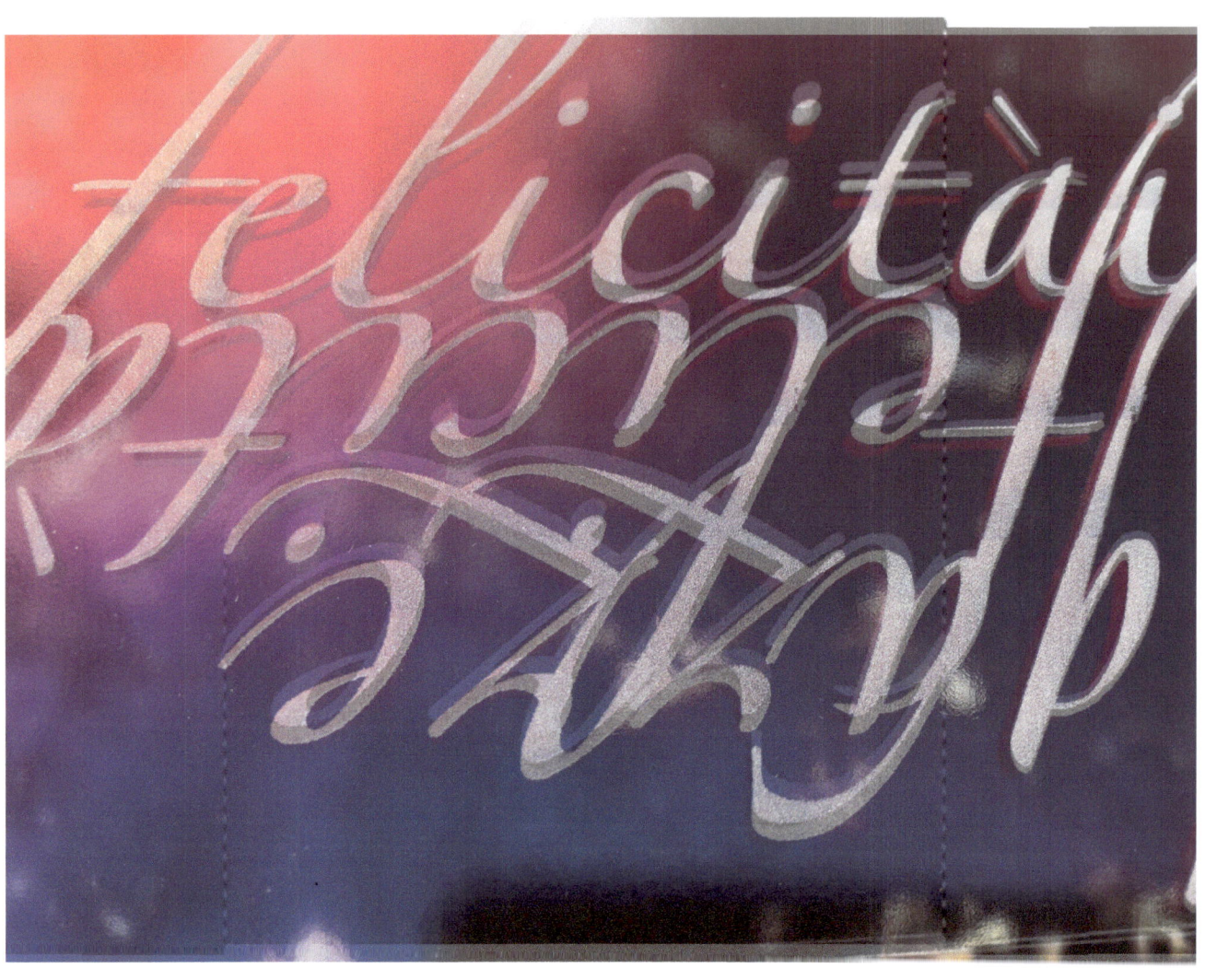

elicita
Honeycomb variation in red and grey, dichroic glass against steel with glass dust halo

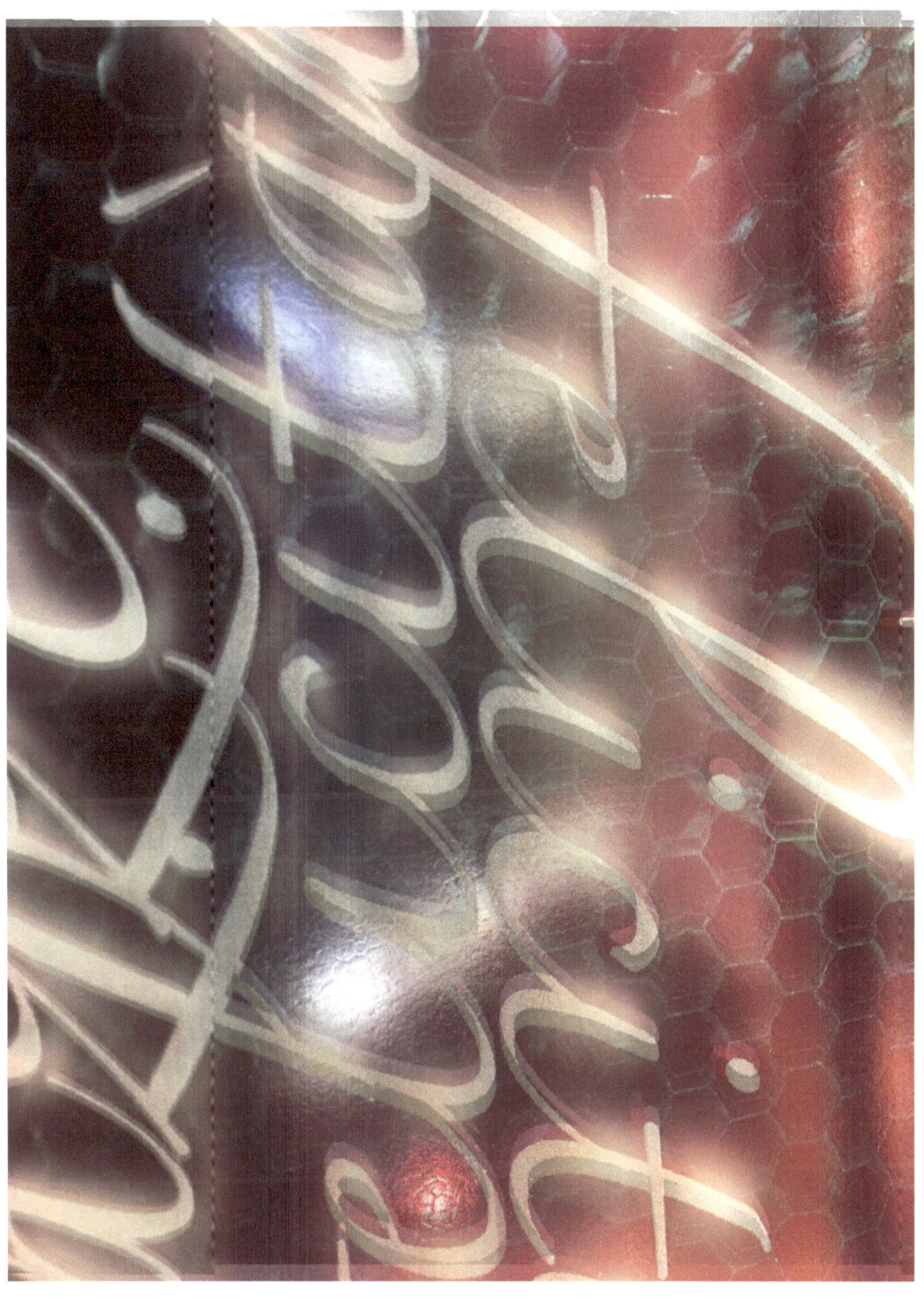

Metaphosphor
Mirror variation, with glass dust halo, reflecting light in MIT lab

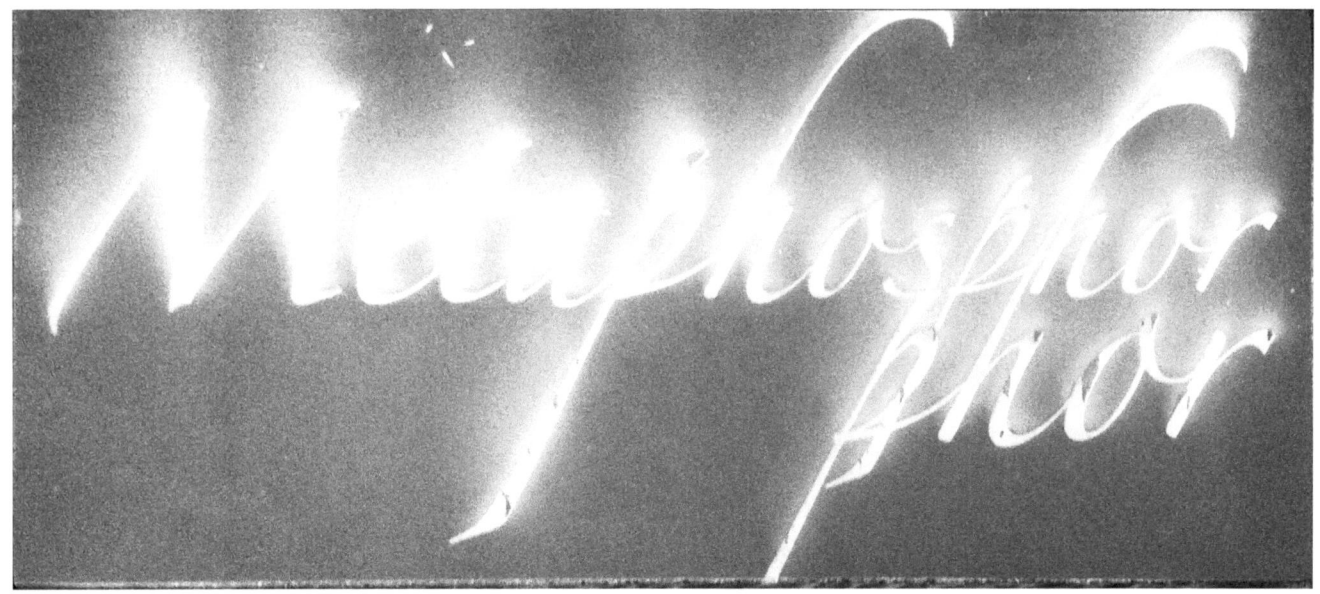

foufoufeullicite, variation #1
Honeycomb variation in black, dichroic glass against steel with glass dust halo

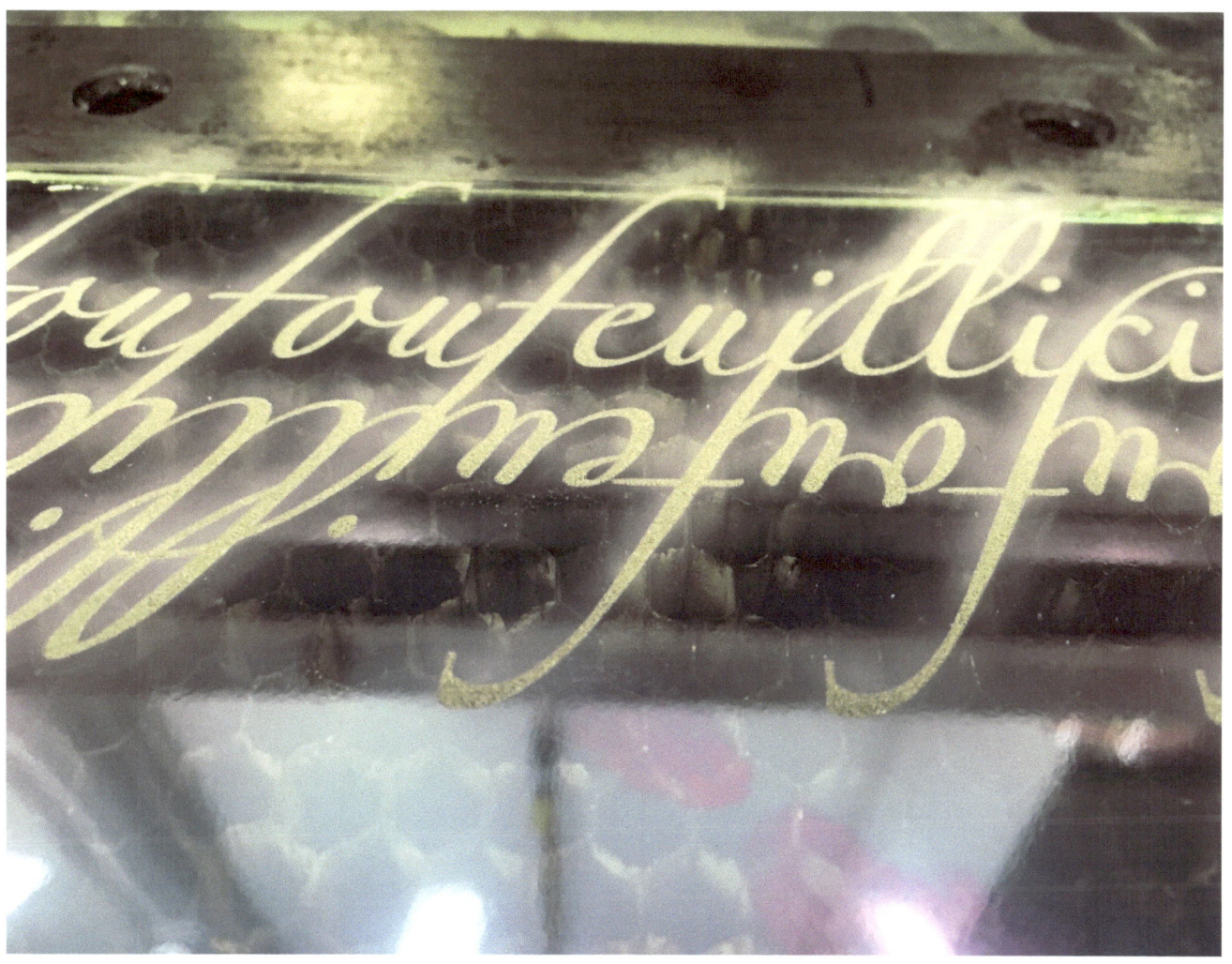

Melonight, variation #2
Red and violet variation, dichroic glass against foil with candlelight

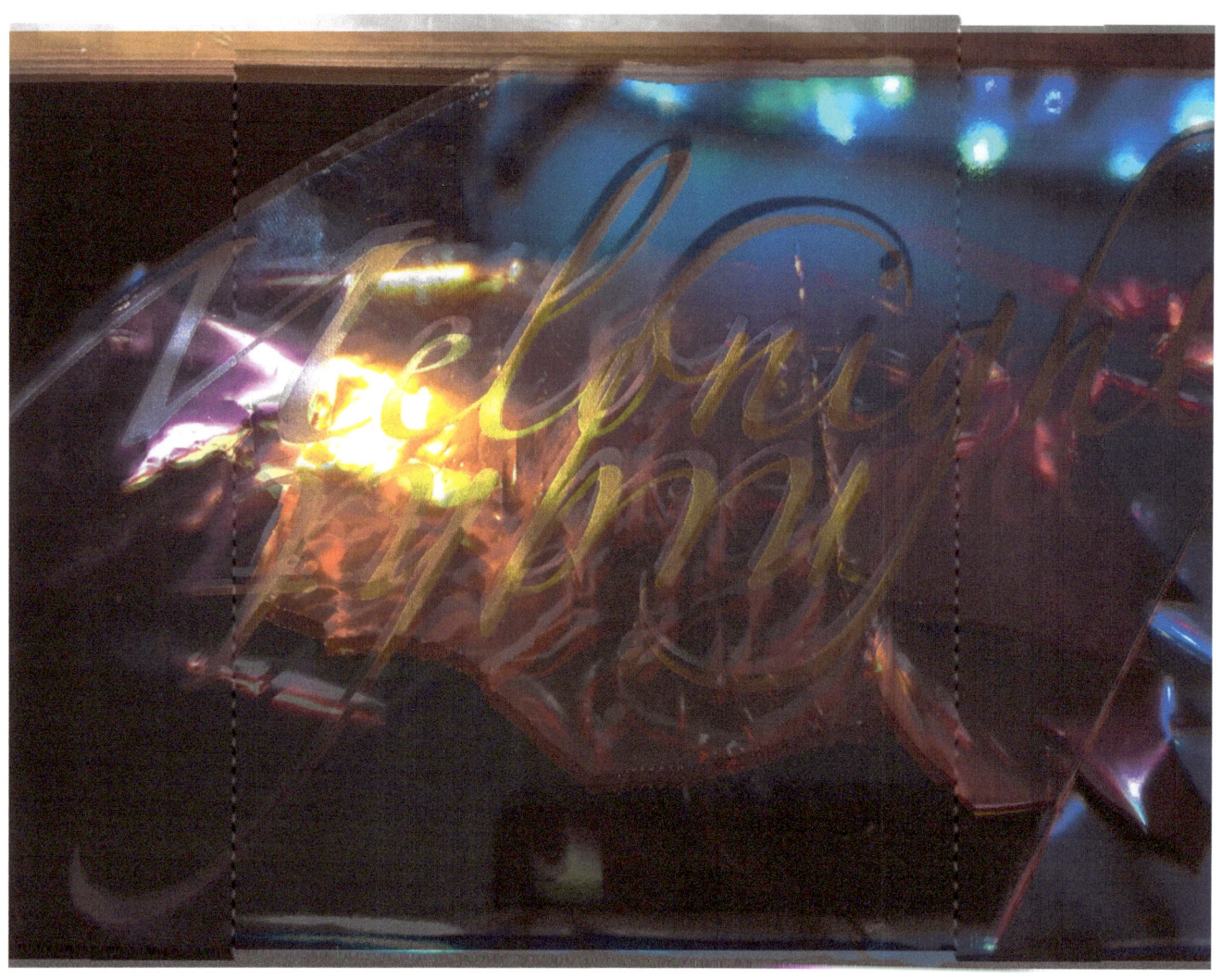

eloni'g
Layered variation in pink, violet, and cerulean, dichroic glass on marble gravestone reflecting sky

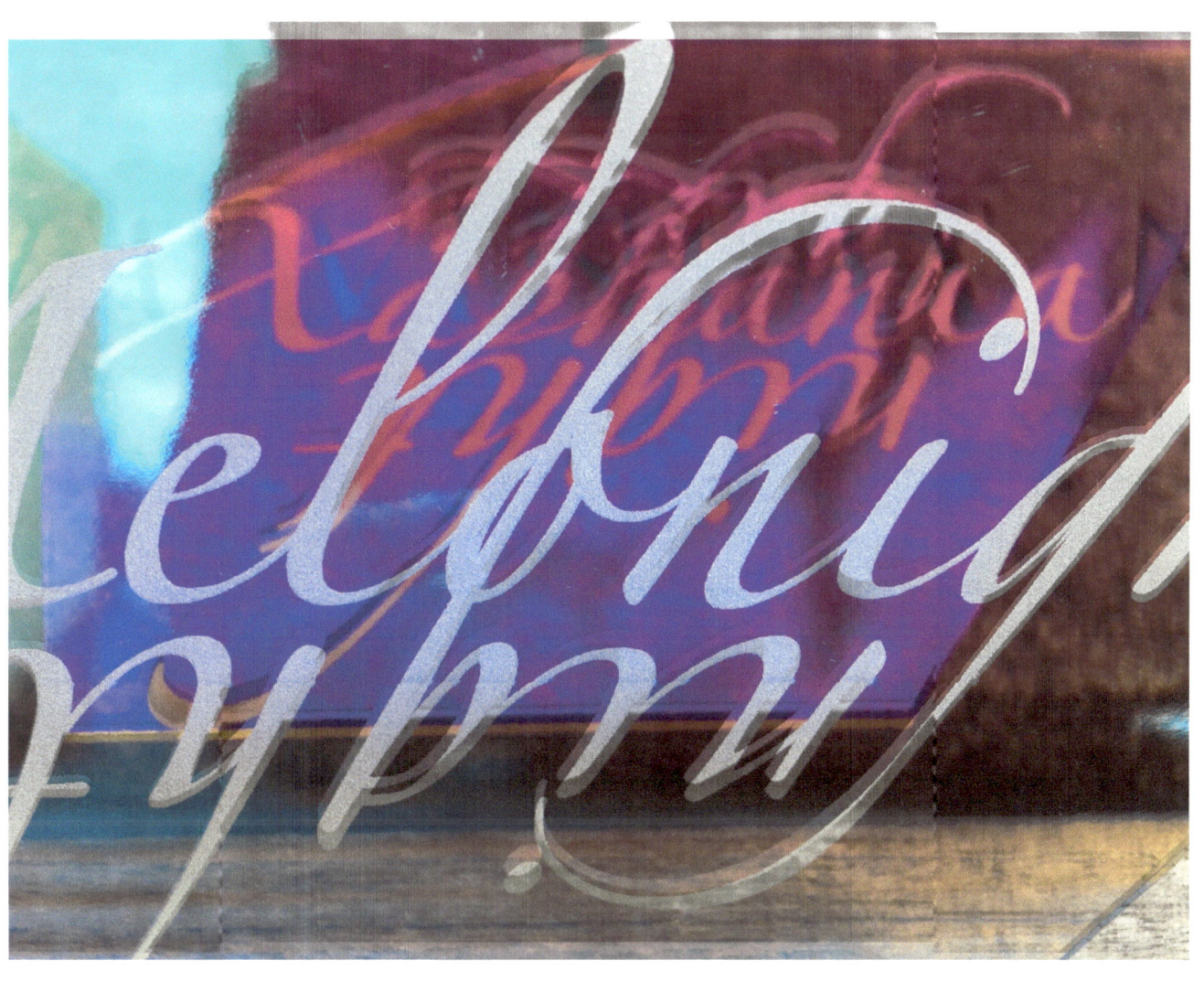

foufoufeuillicite, variation #2
Earth variation, dichroic glass against earth and leaves, reflecting sky and tree branches

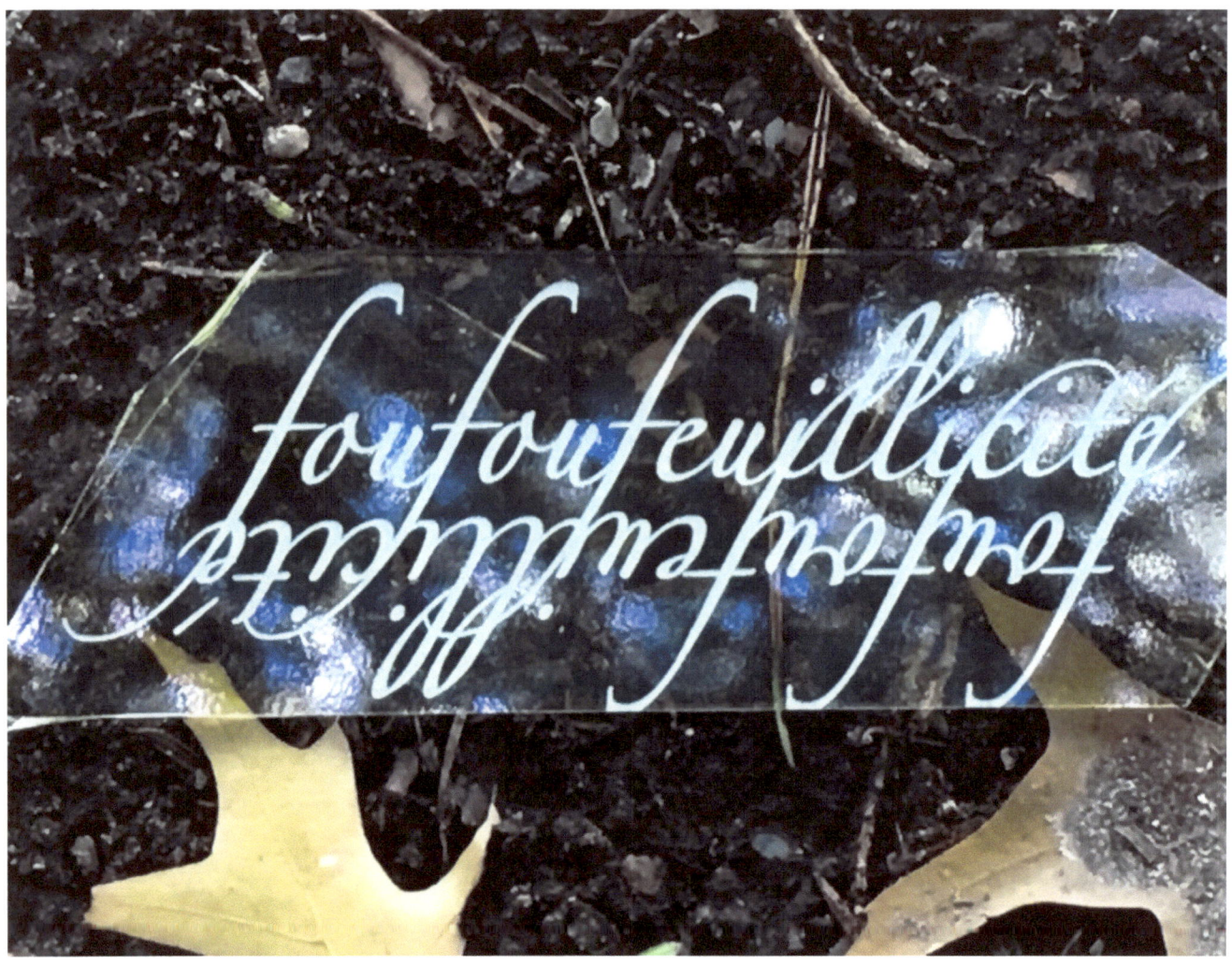

sass'citaci
Rain puddle variation, dichroic glass on mud reflecting sky

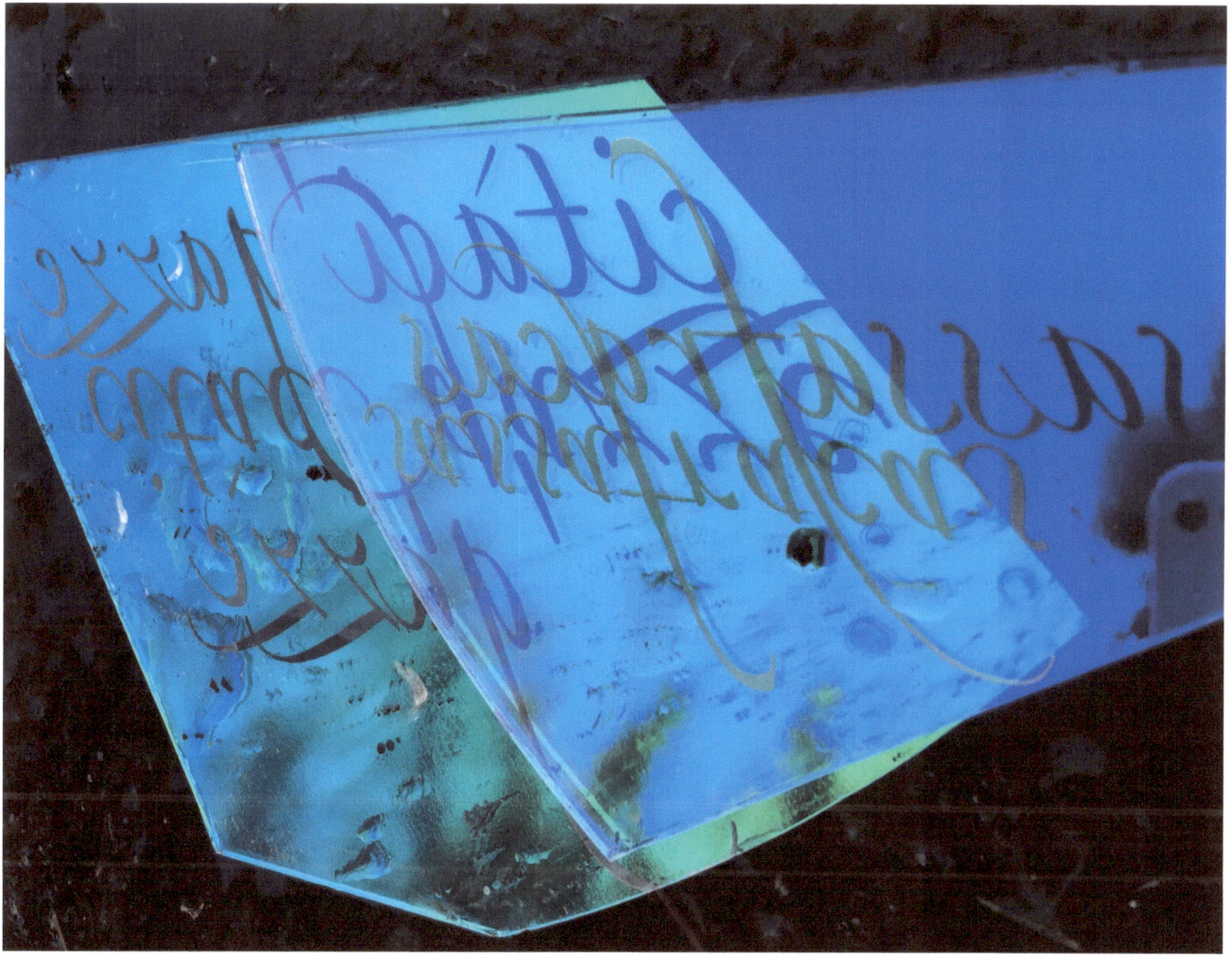

Suzanne Mercury

Inkl'ingthingie
Inked mirror, with glass dust halo reflecting sky

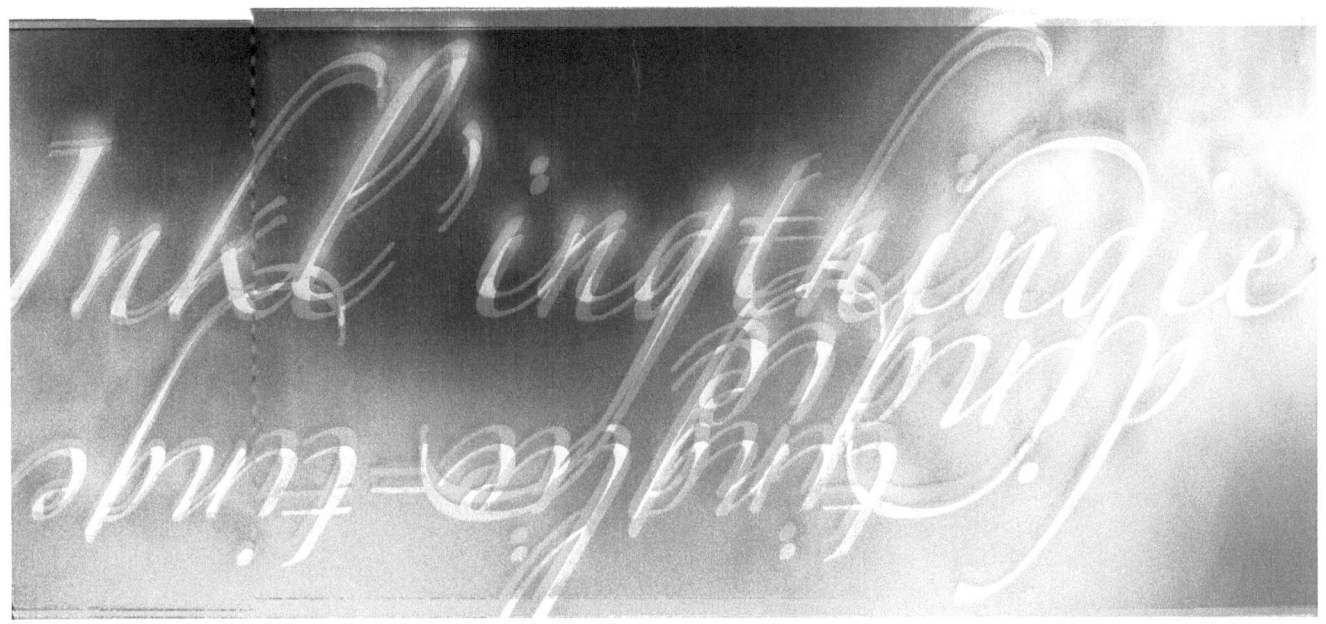

Xaphania, variation #3
Variation in gold, dichroic glass misted with water with hands and houseplants

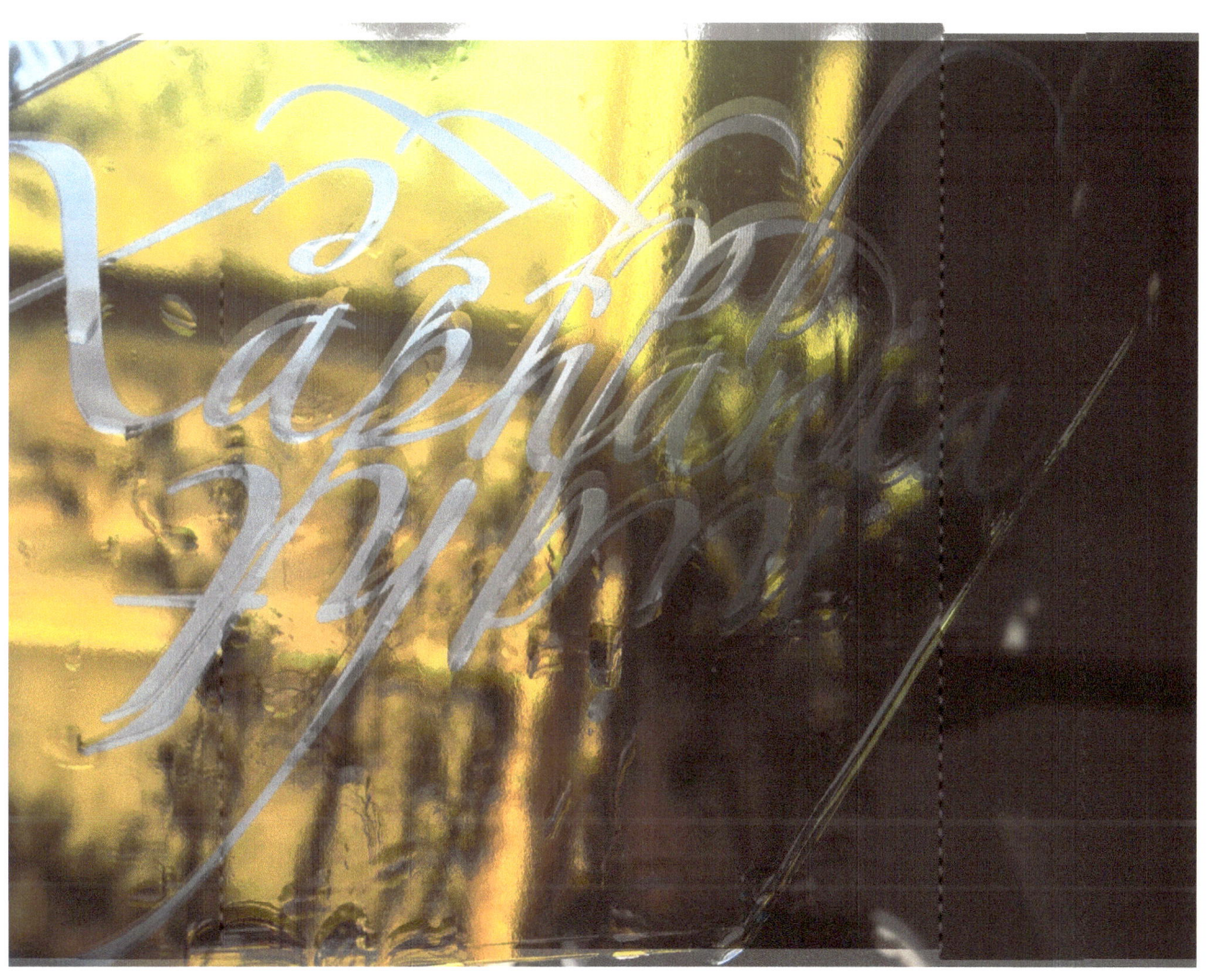

Suzanne Mercury

Xapha'zze
Reverse variation in blue and green, dichroic glass against marble gravestone reflecting afternoon sun and trees

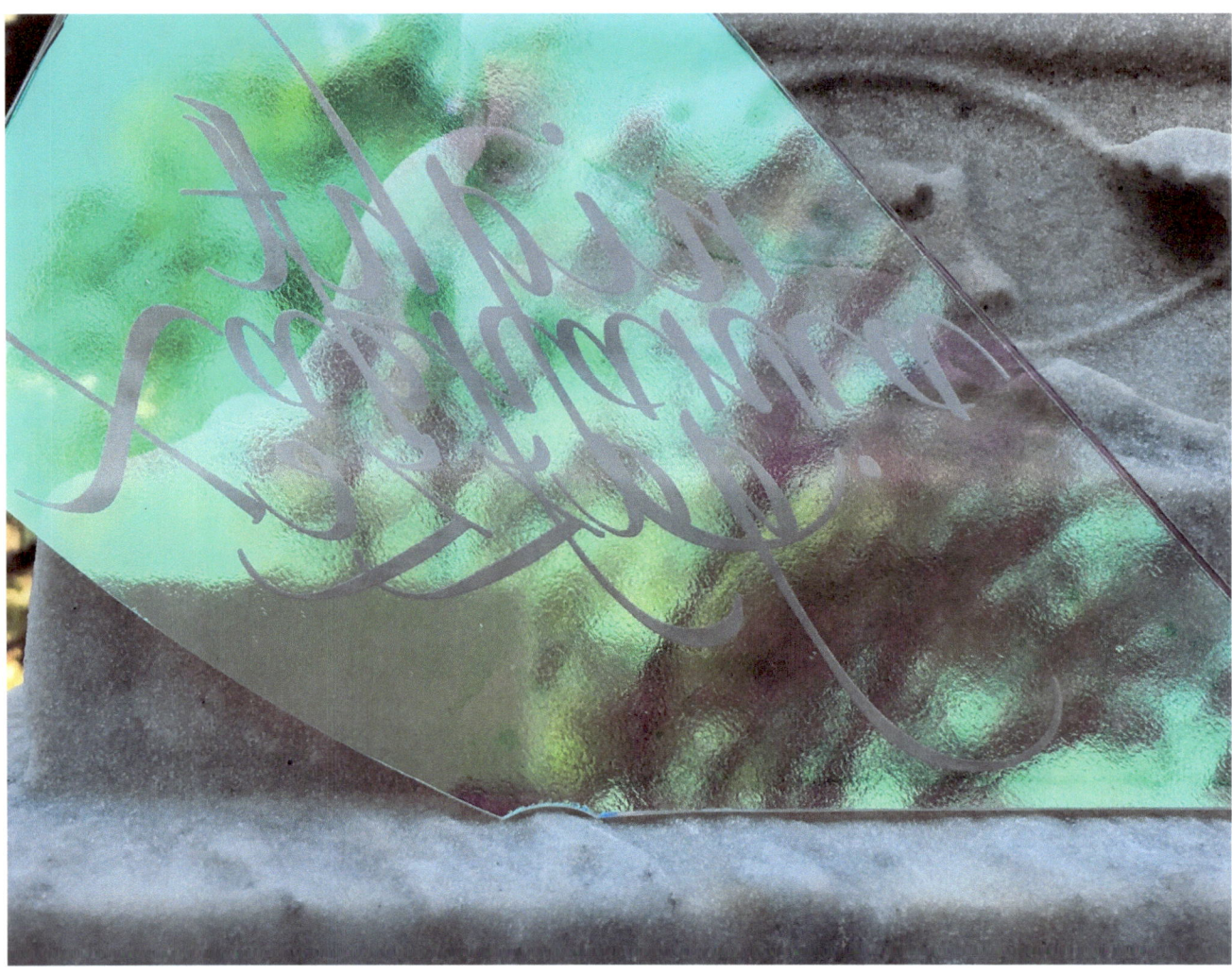

Shards and Earth
Cool light variation, dichroic glass against earth, reflecting sky

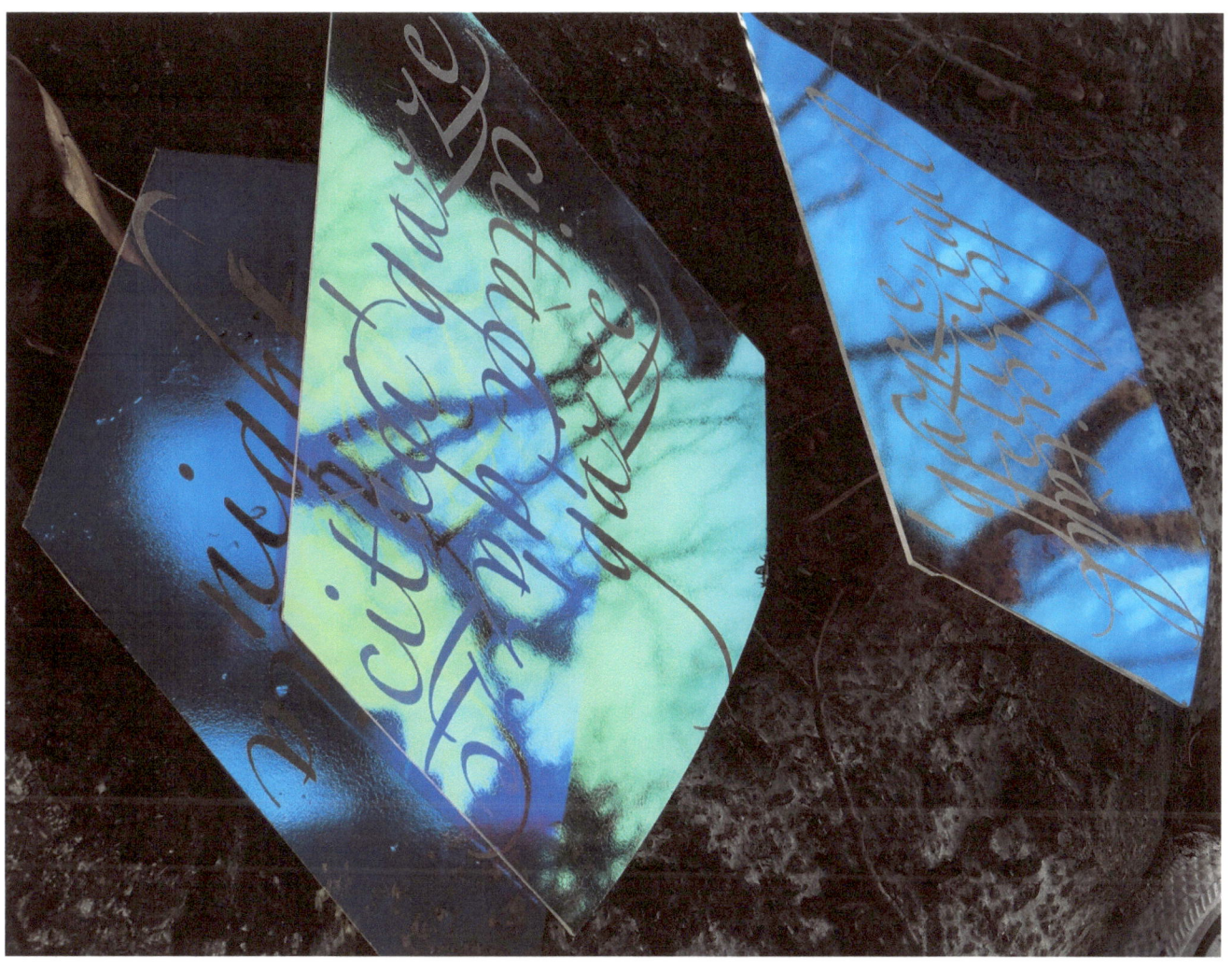

el'tail
Warm light variation, dichroic glass against steel with gold and glass dust halo

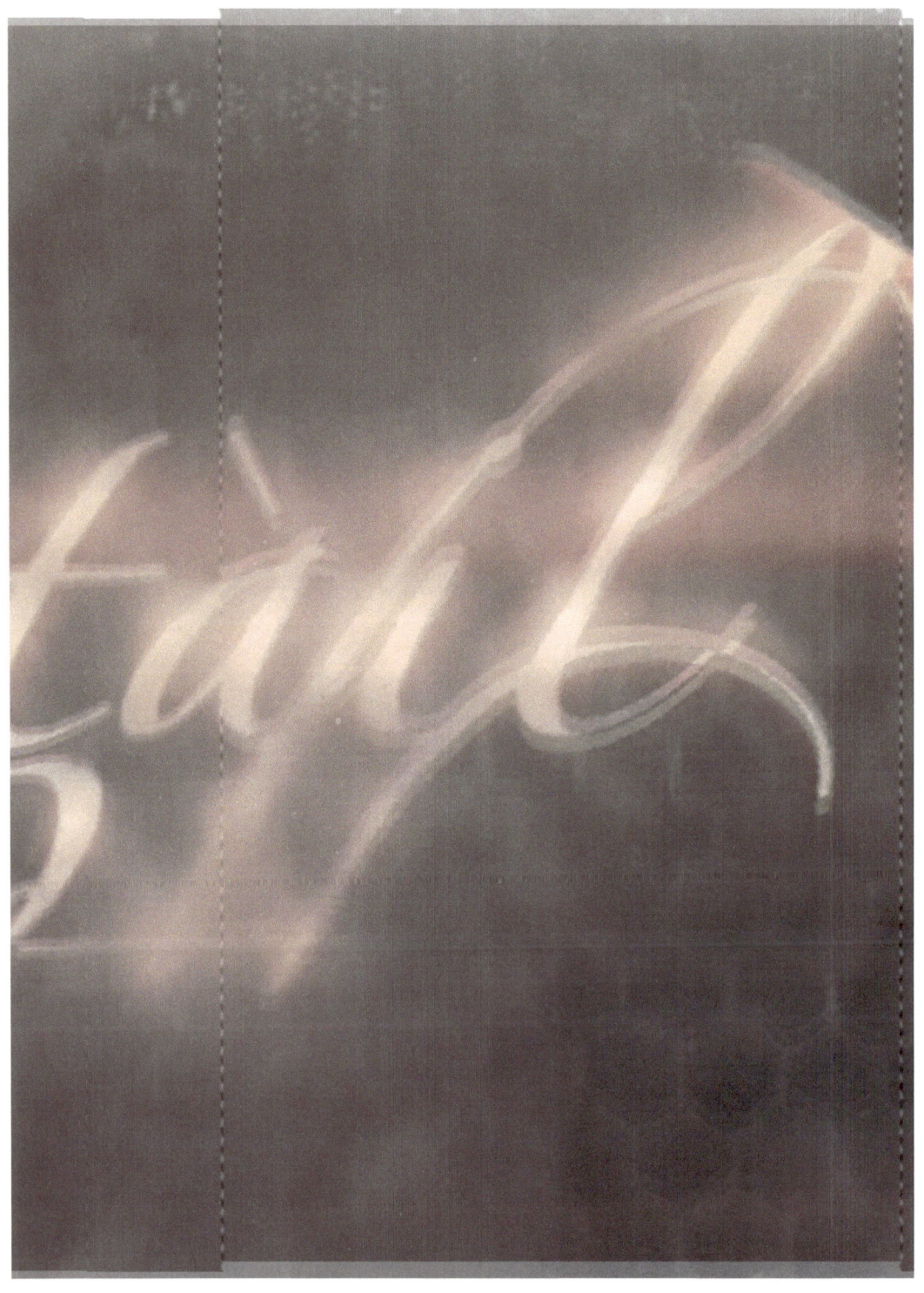

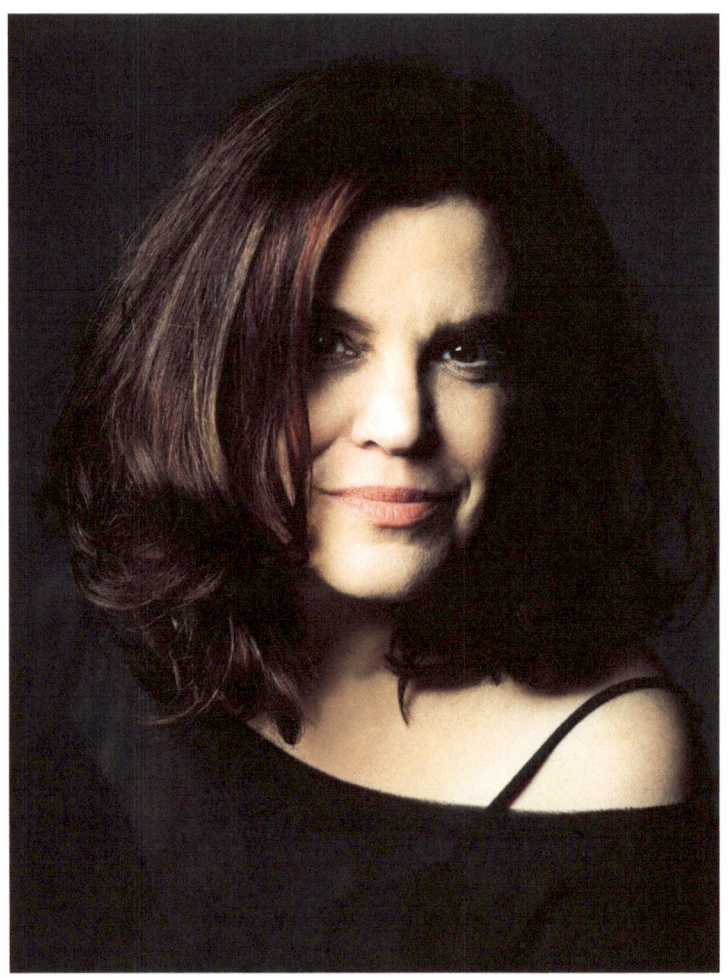

Suzanne Mercury is a poet, impassioned flânuese, gardener, lucid dreamer, and visual artist who creates mixed-media assemblages using found objects, old book pages, LED lights, glass, gold, tree branches, and all manner of natural materials. She publishes tiny books through Jewelweed Press, including her two pwoermds collections, *Meteor'gasmi* and *Silenchanté*.

Suzanne received her MFA in creative writing at Syracuse University, and has published her works in a variety of places including *SpoKe*, *Truck*, *Summer Stock*, *Throg Sludge*, and *Let the Bucket Down*. She has also studied visual art at the School of the Museum of Fine Arts at Tufts as well as landscape history at the Landscape Institute at The Arnold Arboretum of Harvard University. She has shown her work and given readings and performances in Cambridge, Boston, and Istanbul.

www.ingramcontent.com/pod-product-compliance
Lightning Source LLC
Chambersburg PA
CBHW051942210526
45473CB00006B/2345